BUYING ECO FABRICS

FOR FASHION START-UPS

CHRIS WALKER

MY BEST ADVICE

If you are an Eco brand then I recommend you incorporate the story of the Eco factory you are working with into your marketing. This serves two purposes. You make your Eco factory partner visible so your target customers can verify and believe your Eco claims. Secondly, the factory feels ownership in your brand which bodes well for a long term relationship and motivates them to be true to their Eco claims.

This advice is risky for two reasons. The first is that no factory is perfect and there will always be a skeleton in the closet that could come out on social media. Even if the factory is Oeko Tex certified or FairTrade certified, when you visit the factory, I guarantee you will find situations that don't meet your expectations. The second reason is that if your competition finds out where you are producing your Eco products, then they will approach the factory to get their production done there too and now the factory can raise prices to the highest bidder. As an Eco brand you need to be intelligently transparent and mitigate these risks.

. . .

If you don't want to share your supply chain and just say, "Our factories are X, Y and Z certified," then you might be accused of greenwashing. Certificates are easily bought and they are losing their credibility. Don't hide the identity of your factories if you want to stand out as confidently Eco. Let your customers verify your Eco claims themselves. If you choose greenwashing then it's just a matter of time before you get called out. Choose your factories carefully and be transparent. Bite the bullet, incorporate the factory's story into your story.

TABLE OF CONTENTS

46 SOURCES OF ECO FABRICS

Are you an established brand or a start up that wants to buy Eco fabrics in Vietnam and produce your garments here? If yes, this book is for you. I introduce you to 46 sources of Eco fabrics.

There are not many Eco fabric sellers in Vietnam, therefore I have included sources from around the world as well. Their fabrics can be imported into Vietnam for garment production.

In this book I define Eco. I question if there is such a thing as an Eco fabric. I explain how to check if a fabric is Eco. I introduce the basics of fabric dyeing and tell you about future Eco dyeing technologies. Finally, I introduce you to people and companies selling Eco fabric and or sewing services.

If you need mind-numbing details then I recommend the following blogs and books:

- Organicclothing.blogs.com by Michael Lackman
- O Ecotextiles blog by Two Sisters Patty and Leigh Ann

- *Our Stolen Future: Are We Threatening Our Fertility, Intelligence, and Survival?* By Theo Colborn
- *Silent Spring* book by Rachel Carson

Silent Spring should be required reading for all die-hard Eco enthusiasts. In the late 1950s, Rachel Carson turned her attention to conservation, especially environmental problems that she believed were caused by synthetic pesticides. The result was *Silent Spring* (1962.) Her book brought environmental concerns to the American public. *Silent Spring* was met with fierce opposition by chemical companies, but it spurred a reversal in national pesticide policy and it led to a nationwide ban on DDT for agricultural uses. It also inspired an environmental movement that led to the creation of the U.S. Environmental Protection Agency.

ECO INFLUENCERS

Janet Seltzer

Janet Seltzer is a friend of mine who works as a consultant to fashion brands. There are many people like Janet that I met while writing this book. They helped me understand the basics of Eco fabrics and introduced me to sources of Eco fabrics that I'd like to share with you. I dedicate this book to all the people like Janet who are involved in Eco fabric production and who aim to make the world a better place. Here is what I learned from Janet.

Naia™ is a cellulosic yarn made by Eastman Chemical that is taking steps towards becoming Eco. It is a bio-based material that comes from sustainably managed forests and is manufactured in a socially responsible manner in the USA. Naia™ fiber starts from sustainably resourced wood pulp, then is produced in a close looped process with all of its waste either being reused or sold. Any water that is released is scrubbed clean and certified by the USDA BioPreferred Program.

.   .   .

Cupro is another cellulosic yarn with an Eco story that Janet introduced me to. It is a bio-based fiber made from cotton linter. Linter is ultra-fine silky fibers that stick to the seeds of the cotton plant after it has been ginned. Cupro yarn makes silk-like fabric because the yarn does not have striations or markings like normal cotton. Fabric made with Cupro yarn can be machine washed and dried, unlike silk. It is similar to rayon but breathes and regulates body temperature like cotton. It was invented by a German but the production is managed by a Japanese company called Asahi Kasei. Cupro is an example of up-cycling bio-waste into new fabric.

- Email: janetaseltzer@aol.com

Thao Vu

Thao Vu is a dedicated Vietnamese Eco superhero. She does not sell Eco fabric; she produces it for herself. She inspires me and should inspire us all because she is dedicated to being Eco, running a successful business and is home grown in Vietnam.

Thao Vu is a designer, artist and Eco-entrepreneur. She is a leader among the pioneering group of young designers who have made Hanoi an emerging creative fashion hub. She is the founder and designer of Kilomet109, a fashion label that uses and improves native Vietnamese fabric production techniques. The Eco fabrics used in her collections come from Vietnam's ethnic minority groups.

All of her dyeing, weaving, batik drawing and calendering are done by dozens of women artisans in multiple ethnic-minority communities across northern Vietnam. The work is labor-intensive. For example, a single batch of cotton fabric is dipped in indigo dye twice a day over a period of about two months.

· · ·

Thao works in the fields with the minority groups and invests in the crops before they are planted. She experiments with the locals to invent new techniques to explore hand-feels and color shades. She loves trying out new dyeing ingredients, such as yam root, green tea and tree bark to compliment the themes of her collections.

Kilomet109 is named for the distance in kilometers between Hanoi and the village in Thai Binh province where Thao grew up. In the video, Natural Dyeing for Eco Fashion in Vietnam, she introduces some of Vietnam's native natural dyes.

Natural Dyeing for Eco Fashion in Vietnam

If you are aspiring to be an Eco fashion designer running into minimum order quantity (MOQ) barriers and high price points then study Thao Vu's business model, do it locally, don't give up your dedication and be profitable like Thao.

- Email: info@kilomet109.com
- Website: https://kilomet109.com

ECO VS SUSTAINABLE

These three terms eco, eco-friendly and sustainable have the same end goal in mind. It is ok to use them interchangeably.

Eco is short for ecology or ecological. An Eco person values clean water, clean air and clean soil. Something that is Eco preserves clear water, clean air and clean soil.

Eco friendly means not harmful to the environment. The environment includes living things, so Eco friendly means not harmful to living things like fabric mill workers, animals and you.

The best definition of sustainable is development that meets the needs of the present without compromising the ability of future generations to meet their own needs.

In my book I refer to things as Eco and my meaning encompasses all three definitions. It is ok to use them interchangeably. I use one term: Eco. I use a capital E to remind us that my meaning includes all three meanings: eco, eco-friendly and sustainable.

The first question I ask in a conversation about Eco fabrics is, what does Eco mean to you? To me, being Eco is more about decisions people make than the chemicals or technology used to produce fabrics. It is the decisions people will make that will help us sustain 9.7 billion people in 2050. It is decisions that people have made that have gotten us to this point in history where the Earth Overshoot Day is decreasing.

Overshoot Day. What?

Earth Overshoot Day is the date each year when humanity's annual demand on nature exceeds what the Earth can provide in one year. In 2018, Earth Overshoot Day fell on the 1st of August. It is the earliest date since ecological overshoot recording began in the early 1970s. The Global Footprint Network created Overshoot Day. They assert that if we continue to consume at current rates, then in 2030 we will need 2 times the earth's resources each year to maintain our standard of living.

- Website: Overshootday.org

THE MYSTERY OF ECO

Have you heard about beautiful turquoise red rivers around the world? There are some that you don't want to swim in because the colors are poison. Nature-lovers were rather "irked" in April of 2009 when a 150-ft stretch of the River Irk in northwest England was filled with bright white foam up to 10 feet thick. A detergent factory upstream denied responsibility for the situation, stating the cause "remains a mystery."

Eco was a mystery to me before I started researching for this book. From my point of view in Vietnam, there was no such thing as an Eco fabric. I considered all the production steps and asked myself, what is the chance that each step is Eco? Here is a list of fabric production steps:

1. Fiber production
2. Yarn spinning
3. Fabric knitting or weaving
4. Pre-treatment
5. Dyeing or printing
6. Finishing treatments
7. Transporting fabrics to marketplaces

What is the chance that all the organizations involved in these steps are using raw materials and processes that are 100% Eco?

Hazardous chemicals are at the heart of the mystery because they are not easily detected. What is the probability that tests are being done during each production step to check for hazardous chemicals? Here is a list of hazardous chemicals that can be present in fabrics:

- Formaldehyde
- Heavy metals
- Chlorinated phenols
- Azo or allergenic dyestuffs
- Phthalates
- Polycyclic aromatic hydrocarbons
- Perfluorinated compounds
- Tensides

- Pesticides
- Chlorinated benzenes and toluenes
- Dimethyl fumarate
- Organic tin
- Chlorinated paraffins

These are some of the harmful chemicals that disqualify a fabric from being Eco. We should be concerned because they cause cancer and they can mutate our DNA. These chemicals are mysteriously present in our clothing - be aware.

Is any fabric 100% Eco?

Seeking the answer to this question, solving the mystery, is why I decided to write this book. Basically, I threw the BS flag and decided to research it myself. **My answer is no.**

Bamboo fabric is chemically manufactured by "cooking" bamboo shoots in sodium hydroxide and carbon disulfide combined with multi-phase chlorine bleaching.

Organic cotton requires electricity to gin, spin, knit, weave and finish; the electricity is often generated from fossil fuels or nuclear power.

All synthetic fibers are made from petroleum distillation which causes air and water pollution.

Bamboo, organic cotton and recycled polyester fabrics are not 100% Eco.

. . .

The outdoor brand Patagonia is an Eco leader and they sum things up honestly and beautifully, "At Patagonia, we start with the knowledge that everything we produce comes at a cost to the environment. We then work continuously to lower the environmental and social costs of our products at every phase of their life cycle - from improving our manufacturing processes at every level of the supply chain through increasing our use of recycled and natural materials to encouraging reuse, repair and recycling among our customers."

GOTS is the Global Organic Textile Standard. In their guide book they state that it is nearly impossible to produce any fabric in an industrial way without the use of chemical inputs. The GOTS approach is to define criteria for low impact and low residual chemical inputs for dyestuffs, auxiliaries and finishes.

To me the mystery is solved by acknowledging that no fabric is 100% Eco. There are degrees of Eco. Standards like Oeko Tex, bluesign®, GRS and GOTS give us reference points to know the degree to which a fabric is Eco.

Honest and transparent Eco fabric producers are the solution to making the world of fabric production more Eco. They genuinely care about the environment, fabric mill workers, animals and you. They are producing and selling Eco fabric to make the world a better place.

WHY MOST FABRICS ARE NOT 100% ECO

What follows is disturbing information about pollution and animal abuse in the fabric industry and it's important. Be informed and get motivated to make things right. The things I learned while writing this book seriously scare me. Read this chapter and get motivated to be intelligently Eco. Here is ground zero.

Cotton pesticides

Cotton has excellent absorbency, durability, and intrinsic softness. It accounts for over 50% of all clothing produced worldwide. Cotton covers 2.5% of the world's cultivated land and uses 16% of the world's pesticides. Pesticides include herbicides, insecticides, and defoliants. The pesticides used to increase crop yields are polluting ground water and causing serious health issues in animals and humans.

Aldicarb (also known as Temik) is a carbamate insecticide used in cotton fields around the world - it's toxic. An outbreak of aldicarb poisoning sickened more than 2,000 people who had eaten California watermelons. Another case was when 288 of 318 sheep died in south central Washington State when they grazed on land over-sprayed with Aldicarb. Despite intentions to ban Aldicarb by the US Environmental Protection Agency (EPA) it is still used in the US with a new name: AgLogic 15G.

DDT is an insecticide used in cotton farming - it's toxic. DDT has been shown to cause cancer in laboratory animals. People exposed to DDT report a prickling sensation of the mouth, nausea, dizziness, confusion, headache, lethargy, incoordination, vomiting, fatigue, and tremors. In 1973 the EPA banned DDT in the US. China stopped producing DDT in 2007. India still produces DDT and uses it to control mosquitos from spreading diseases like malaria.

RoundUp contains glyphosate which is a herbicide used in cotton production to kill weeds - it's toxic. Millions of liters of glyphosate herbicide have been sprayed over half of Argentina's cultivated land. Since the Argentinian government approved spraying in 1996 residents and doctors reported high rates of birth defects as well as infertility, stillbirths, miscarriages, and cancers. Pablo Ernesto Piovano is a documentary photographer who captured images of people affected by the spraying of glyphosate in Argentina. He titled the project: Human Cost of Agrotoxins. Glyphosate is not banned by the U.S. or E.U. governments. Cotton growers use RoundUp to control weeds.

Photo by Pablo Ernesto Piovano. Human Costs of Agrotoxins.

DEF6, Folex and Tribufos are defoliants used to improve cotton crop yields - they are toxic. They make cotton leaves fall off the cotton blossom to make it easier to get to the cotton fibers. Agent Orange is a famous defoliant used by the U.S. in the Vietnam War to deprive the enemy of food crops and cover. Agent orange damages genes, resulting in deformities among the offspring of exposed victims. Exposed veterans, both US and Vietnamese, developed serious health problems.

Cotton is considered the world's dirtiest crop due to its heavy use of pesticides like DDT, Aldicarb, Roundup and Folex. Cotton fabrics are not 100% Eco.

Rayon, viscose, modal, lyocell, Tencel®, and bamboo

All of these yarns are made from regenerated cellulosic fiber. Cellulose is the most abundant organic polymer on Earth. It is a structural component in the cell walls of all green plants. Most cellulosic fiber is derived from wood pulp. Wood has an average cellulosic content of 40%. Bamboo has 45% cellulose. All these fibers are referred to as regenerated cellulosic fibers because natural raw cellulose is cooked in chemical soup that contains sodium hydroxide and carbon disulfide. The process is called hydrolysis alkalization.

Rayon is the first generation of cellulosic fibers. Rayon is also known as viscose. Modal is the second generation of cellulosic fibers. Lyocell is third generation of cellulosic fibers. Tencel® is Lenzing's brand name for lyocell.

The problem with regenerated cellulosic fibers are the chemical used to make them, namely sodium hydroxide and carbon disulfide. Skin contact with sodium hydroxide causes pain, redness, burns, and blistering. Eye contact causes severe burns with redness, swelling, pain and blurred vision. Ingestion burns the lips, tongue, throat and stomach. Symptoms of sodium hydroxide poisoning include nausea, vomiting, stomach cramps and diarrhea. Severe exposure can cause blindness and death.

Carbon disulfide is extremely flammable and causes eye, skin, and respiratory tract irritation. If ingested it causes convulsions, seizures and possible coma. Carbon disulfide causes adverse reproductive and fetal effects in animals. It can cause neural disorders in workers at rayon factories.

There are two ways to "cook" the cellulosic pulp: open loop cooking and closed loop cooking. Open loop cooking is the least Eco because waste is released to the environment. Closed loop cooking is more Eco because the toxic chemicals are recycled and the amount of waste released to the environment is significantly decreased.

If you are using any of these cellulosic fibers and calling them Eco then I recommend you make sure the fibers are made in a factory with **closed loop processes** and **certified waste** water treatment methods. Bottom line is that rayon, viscose, modal, lyocell, Tencel® and bamboo are not 100% Eco.

The best articles I found that tell the detailed story of regenerated cellulosic fibers are on the Organic Clothing Blog and the OEcoTextiles Blog. I highly recommend reading both.

- Website: http://organicclothing.blogs.com
- Website: https://oecotextiles.wordpress.com

Question: if bamboo pulp is used to make rayon and we call it bamboo fabric, then if wood pulp is used to make rayon, then can we call it wood fabric?

When hemp loses its Eco

Hemp, flax, ramie and jute are all bast fibers. Bast fiber is plant fiber collected from inner bark. Bast fibers provide strength to the stem of plants. When removed from the plant, the bast fibers are made into yarn and then fabric. Compared to the rayons mentioned above, chemicals are not needed to harvest bast fibers.

The traditional production of hemp, flax, ramie and jute requires mechanical processes. The three basic processes are retting, decortication and heckling. Retting is the process of separating the fiber from the stalk. The stalks are soaked in water where bacteria release enzymes that naturally start to separate bast fibers from the woody core. After retting, decortication physically removes the tough woody interior from the softer, fibrous exterior of the stalk. Heckling prepares the fibers to be spun into yarn. Heckling splits and straightens the bast fibers and then removes the fibrous core and impurities. The process is 100% Eco. So, what's the problem? The hand-feel is rough.

To achieve a smoother hand-feel on hemp, flax, ramie and jute fabric there are two options: combine the bast fiber yarns with other yarns like cotton, spandex or rayon, or use the cellulose in the bast fibers to make rayon by cooking them in chemicals. Bast fibers lose their Eco when cooked in chemicals and turned into rayon.

Silk mass executions

Silk filament is a continuous thread of great tensile strength measuring from 500 to 1,500 meters. In woven silk, the fiber's triangular structure acts as a prism that refracts light, giving silk its highly prized natural shimmer. So what's the problem?

Silk is Eco except for one major problem. To make one pound of silk, 2,600 silkworms must be executed. Their life begins as a silkworm (caterpillar) and ends as a winged moth. They are killed prematurely and the story is interesting.

Silk has been around since 2,900 BC. During thousands of years of captive breeding, the silkworm has evolved into an invalid. Silkworms live for about 65 days. They voraciously eat mulberry leaves almost non-stop, increasing its weight 10,000 times from a tiny speck to a fat silkworm. When the silkworm is fully grown, it climbs a twig and begins spinning a cocoon of silk around itself. The silkworm transforms into a moth inside the cocoon. It is blind, cannot fly and cannot eat. It only lives a few days as a moth during which time it lays about 500 eggs. The moth pokes a hole in the silk cocoon to get out. Silk farmers don't want to damage the continuous strand of silk so they mass execute the moths by putting them in boiling water or hot ovens. So, when you take into account the mass executions of moths, is silk Eco?

Enter peace silk or vegetarian silk. There are farmers who don't kill moths prematurely and allow the moths to break the silk fibers into smaller staple fibers. These smaller fibers are spun into yarn just like cotton is spun. Peace silk or vegetarian silk is more Eco than filament silk.

Angora rabbit and goat farmers got caught by PETA

People for the Ethical Treatment of Animals (PETA) is the largest animal rights organization in the world. They have more than 6.5 million members and supporters. They all have GoPros.

Angora rabbit farmers who produce Angora Wool got caught on camera. Angora fiber refers to the fur produced by the Angora rabbit. Angora fiber is known for its silky softness, thin fibers, and what knitters refer to as a halo (fluffiness). The Angora rabbit grows hair twice as fast as other rabbits. They are raised in semi-darkness with hair removed every three months. A single rabbit can produce about 1.5kg of fiber per year. The problem is, although it is possible to harvest the fiber from an Angora rabbit by shearing, the small size of the rabbit makes this a time-consuming task. Large-scale commercial Angora fiber production in China favors ripping the fur from their skin several times during their short, abused lives. The undercover video released by PETA shows the rabbits screaming as their fur is ripped from their skin. Is Angora Wool 100% Eco? If sheared then yes, but if ripped then no.

More animal abuse was caught on camera in South Africa. Mohair fabric is produced from Angora goats. The fiber is softer and shinier than wool. Mohair fiber has scales like wool, but the scales are not fully developed. Mohair fabric is hypoallergenic. Its nickname is diamond fiber. So, what's the problem?

Using hidden cameras on 12 South African farms, PETA captured the atrocious conditions that some goats live in, not to mention the brutality they endure during transportation and shearing. Topshop, Gap, H&M and Zara said they would ban mohair garments after footage released by PETA showed the animals being violently handled and mutilated at farms in South Africa. Eco? Not when you include humane treatment of animals in your definition.

What's the skinny on wool?

Wool has many amazing natural properties like natural insulation, water absorbency, mildew and mold resistance, water repellency, durability and fire retardancy. So what's the problem?

When wool is shorn it must be washed to remove dirt and oils from the sheep's sweat. The detergents used to wash the wool include alkylphenol ethoxylates (APEOs.) APEOs are endocrine disruptors. Our endocrine system includes chemical messengers that make sure our body works the way it should. If our endocrine system isn't healthy, we might have problems during puberty or pregnancy. We also might gain weight easily, have weak bones, or lack energy. APEOs are known to be very toxic for aquatic life – there is evidence of male fish transforming into females and crocodile penises decreasing in size. APEO chemicals are used to wash wool and dye fabrics.

The surface of wool fiber has small barbed scales. They are the reason that untreated wool itches. Because of this, wool undergoes descaling treatments and is given a thin polymer coating. Unfortunately, this descaling treatment results in waste water with unacceptably high levels of adsorbable organohalogens (AOX) which are not Eco because they lead to genetic mutations in our bodies.

Last point about wool: mulesing is a surgical procedure performed on sheep and it's painful. The goal of the procedure is to prevent flystrike. Flystrike is a very painful condition where flies lay their eggs under the sheeps' skin and, when the eggs hatch, the hatchlings eat the sheep's tissue. Mulesing spares the sheep this nasty experience. This surgical procedure removes large strips of skin from the buttocks of the animals. Mulesing is performed without any antiseptic, anaesthetic or pain relief in the majority of cases. It is considered an inhumane and unnecessary procedure by many veterinary experts, animal rights activists, sheep breeders, clothing companies and consumers around the world. However, sheep farmers consider it a necessity to ensure the production of affordable merino wool in large quantities. Wool is not 100% Eco.

Cashmere desertification

Cashmere wool comes from goats originating from the Kashmir region in the north of India. Cashmere wool is finer, stronger, lighter, softer, and approximately three times more insulating than sheep wool. Quality cashmere will not pill, will keep its form for years and can be hand-washed - no need for dry-cleaning. And, thanks to China's massive cashmere production efforts, the price of cashmere products has come down to Walmart levels. So, what's the problem?

The grass that the goats eat is gone due to the increase in cashmere goat populations along the northern border of China near Mongolia. The cashmere goats have eaten the grasslands bare and their hooves have destroyed the protective topsoils. The result is desertification that is leading to severe dust storms which are snatched up by winds and carried to the coastal industrial zones of China. There, the Chinese industrial zone pollution mixes with the dust and then flies over to the U.S. within five days. This article in the Chicago Tribune is a great read and tells this desertification story in interesting detail. Cashmere is not 100% Eco.

Recycled synthetics are not 100% Eco

What do polyester, polyethylene, nylon, spandex, acrylic and acetate have in common? They are all fibers used to make synthetic fabrics. They are all made from crude oil and not Eco even if they are recycled.

Crude oil goes through multiple transformations during the refining process. Sulphur dioxide, nitrogen oxide and carbon dioxide gases are released and pollute the air we breathe as a result of refining. These gases contribute to acid rain and to the greenhouse effect. Even if they are recycled from plastic bottles, synthetic fibers are not 100% Eco.

Heard about microfiber pollution?

Synthetic fibers like polyester, polyethylene, nylon, spandex, acrylic and acetate are the source of microfiber pollution. Scientists have discovered large quantities of plastic microfibers in the ocean, on land and in living things. These microfibers have broken off from synthetic fabrics in our wash machines and gotten past sewage plant filters. It is estimated that 700,000 microfibers are released each time 6 kgs of synthetic fabric garments are washed. These microfibers get into the ocean and are consumed by the fish we eat. How much plastic is in your gut? Watch this Youtube video called The Story of Microfiber which describes microfiber pollution in the ocean clearly, or read about ecologist Mark Browne, he is a leader in microfiber pollution research.

Functional fabric folly

Functional fabric properties like dry-fit, cool-air or clima-cool, are hazardous chemicals impregnated into fabrics that rest on our skin. Brands will spin the story any way they can to make you believe their new inventions are harmless. REI, a well know outdoor brand, explains the magic on their website like this: "Moisture wicking relies on capillary action which is the movement of a liquid through tiny spaces within a fabric due to the molecular forces between the liquid and the fabric's internal surfaces. Brands apply a variety of treatments to surfaces within that structure. Don't sweat the science though, just look for the magic phrase - moisture wicking." What they don't tell you is that the magic is actually bad for our health because of chemicals like Triclosan.

Triclosan is used as a coating in anti-bacterial garments. It is banned in the U.S. from consumer soaps, and will no longer be allowed in antiseptic products used in hospitals and other health care settings. Triclosan is suspected to be an endocrine disruptor and toxic for the liver. Evidence is mounting that triclosan causes antibiotic resistance.

Formaldehyde is a flammable, colorless gas with a pungent, suffocating odor you might remember from your biology lab in school. The fabric industry adds formaldehyde to fabric to give anti-cling, anti-static, anti-wrinkle, and anti-shrink functionality. It is also used for permanent pressing, waterproofing, stain resisting, perspiration proofing, moth preventing, mildew resisting and color-fastening. Sounds awesome and helps increase sales really well. Problem is that when applied heavily on garments, formaldehyde can cause skin rashes, bloody noses, lightheadedness, red eyes, and cracked lips. More alarming is that medical studies have linked formaldehyde exposure with nasal cancer and leukemia. The International Agency for Research on Cancer (IARC) classifies formaldehyde as a human carcinogen.

People concerned about chemical overloads should be "anti-" any garment that is advertised as being anti-shrink, anti-bacterial, antimicrobial, anti-static, anti-odor, anti-flame, anti-wrinkle, or anti-stain. In small amounts, these chemicals like triclosan and formaldehyde won't make you drop dead, but we can live healthier without them. Functional fabric is far from Eco.

All negative? Where's the positive?

The positive starts with people making decisions. Learn more about Eco initiatives like Puma's Bring Me Back program. Join Eco organizations like the Sustainable Apparel Coalition or Outdoor Industry Association. Decide to buy products that have a high degree of Eco by using the Good on You App. If you are a manufacturer then choose technology that is the most Eco. If you are a middleman then buy from trusted Eco sources that you personally verified. The bottom line is that no fabric is 100% Eco. There are degrees of Eco and the degrees are determined by the choices people make. The positive is that we have choices and we all can act.

We have come a long way

Watch this video called How Nylon is Made: "Synthetic Fibers: Nylon and Rayon" 1949 Encyclopaedia Britannica Films. I watched a lot of videos about Eco fabrics during my research, this video is by far the most revealing and insightful. It gives a clear explanation of how synthetic fibers, like rayon, are made. It shows footage of working conditions inside an American factory with workers sticking their hands in big chemical baths and breathing what back then were considered harmless fumes. It's ironic how the film glorifies synthetic fibers. The industry has come a long way and is improving. I hope the information in this chapter motivates you to be intelligently Eco.

HOW TO CHECK ECO

Why is it important to learn about certifying bodies and owners of standards? First, we need help from experts to prove degrees of Eco. Second, these certifying bodies and owners of standards can introduce us directly to sellers of Eco fabrics.

Owners of standards define and update criteria that must be met to qualify as Eco. Examples are Oeko Tex, GOTS, Blue Sign, GRS and AFIRM.

MCL Global is the leading publication platform for the global apparel industry. They published the Textile Standards & Legislation back in 2008. Their website, TextileStandards.com, offers a searchable online database of over 70 standards. If you want your business to comply with the relevant social and environmental standards, minimize risk in your supply chain and avoid damage to your brand reputation, then this list will help you find the best standard.

. . .

Certifying bodies know the standards backwards and forwards. They test in laboratories or go out in the field to ensure that the standards are being met. Examples are Control Union, SGS and Intertek.

What follows is introductory information and contacts for some certifying bodies and owners of standards in Vietnam.

Hohenstein Institute (Oeko-Tex)

Hohenstein Institute is both the owner of standards and the certifying body of their standards. They have many complicated standards. Here are three:

- **EcoPassport** standard focuses on controlling the input to the production process. EcoPassport verifies that all the chemicals used at the beginning of the production process are Eco.
- **STeP** standard verifies that all the production steps are Eco.
- **Standard 100** certifies the end product is Eco. If any garment is produced from a Oeko Tex Standard 100 certified factory, then it can be tested for a list of harmful substances. If the tests pass then none of the harmful substances should be present.

There are approximately 300 Standard 100 factories and 3 STeP certified factories in Vietnam. Germany.vn has a list of factories in Vietnam that are certified by Hohenstein. You can also find a world wide list at Oeko-tex.com. Here are the 3 STeP certified factories in Vietnam:

- Bac Giang - http://bgg.vn
- Tex-Giang - http://tex-giang.com.vn
- Midori Apparel - https://www.midori-anzen.co.jp

Hohenstein is unique because it is both the owner of standards and the only official certifying body for those standards. There is only one lab in Germany that is authorized to certify (test) the results with their official Oeko-tex stamp of approval. Hohenstein certified products are randomly selected from retailers around the world and tested by the Hohenstein lab. If the random tests fail, then the certified factory that produced the garments has one week to explain, remedy and resend samples for testing.

For more information contact Mr. Tran, the country manager for Hohenstein Institute.

- Email: vietnam@hohenstein.com
- Website: https://germany.vn

Global Organic Textile Standard (GOTS)

GOTS is just the owner of a standard. Their standard is outlined in their GOTS Standard 5.0 manual which you can download from their website.

GOTS was introduced in 2006. It is the leading standard for the processing of fabric and apparel using organic fibers. It has gained universal recognition and replaced many previous standards. The standard includes environmentally and socially oriented criteria. In 2016 there were 4,642 certified GOTS facilities around the world.

. . .

GOTS has a public database of certified factories. Here are three companies selling GOTS certified products in Vietnam:

- Xindadong Textiles - xindadongdenim.com
- Mei Sheng Textiles - meisheng.meishengtextilesgroup.com
- Far Eastern Polytex - facebook.com/Polytex2016/

Here is what you can expect to achieve with GOTS certification. At least 70% of the fibers are organically grown. The use of chemicals that cause cancer, birth defects and other serious illnesses is prohibited. Only low impact chemicals are permitted. The standards manual clearly lists all the chemicals that are prohibited. GOTS also includes stringent restrictions on waste water treatment and requires producers to have targets and procedures to reduce energy consumption. Social standards must be met and are based on the key norms of the International Labour Organization. Examples of key norms are safe working conditions, no discrimination and no child labour in the factories. Regular inspections are conducted by independent certifiers along the entire apparel supply chain to protect the reputation of GOTS certification.

There are no GOTS representatives in Vietnam. Felicia Shi is a contact person in China.

- Email: felicia@global-standard.org

bluesign®

The bluesign® standard focuses on fabric production steps. The Switzerland-based organization, officially known as Bluesign Technologies AG, provides independent auditing of fabric mills, examines manufacturing processes and audits raw materials and energy usage. What makes the bluesign® system so unique? By using an input stream management approach, harmful substances are eliminated from the beginning. Other standards certify finished products by end-sample testing. Within the bluesign® system all chemical inputs undergo a risk assessment based on best available technique (BAT) and advice is given to the industry to minimize the risk to people and the environment. Currently there are four bluesign® partner companies in Vietnam:

- Designer Textiles - www.designertextiles.co.nz
- Huge Bamboo - www.hugebamboo.net
- Saitex - www.sai-tex.com
- Tiong Liong - www.vntioliong.com

Six more are going through the bluesign® screening process. bluesign® does not have a representative in Vietnam. Ellen Tse is a contact person in Hong Kong.

- Email: ellen_tse@bluesign.com

Global Recycled Standard

The Global Recycled Standard (GRS) is intended for companies making and/or selling products with recycled content of any fiber type. If you are using recycled polyester then you need to know about the GRS standard. GRS was originally developed by a certifying body called Control Union in 2008. Ownership of the GRS was passed to the Textile Exchange on 1 January 2011. GRS ensures water treatment is in place, no toxic additives are used as process chemicals, no finishes such as fire retardants or stain repellants are added, and that workers have basic rights. GRS stipulates that the amount of recycled content must be at least 20%. It provides a track and trace certification system that ensures that the recycled claim is true. The details of the GRS standard are in their GRS 4.0 manual.

- Website: https://textileexchange.org

I searched their database of factories in Vietnam that sell GRS certified recycled products.

- Century - www.theky.vn
- Chyang Sheng - www.csgroup-vn.com
- Formosa - LinkedIn
- Formosa Taffeta - www.ftc.com.tw
- Huge Bamboo - www.hugebamboo.net
- Pan Textile - pantextile.com.vn

AFIRM

AFIRM is the apparel and footwear international Restricted Substance List (RSL) management working group. AFIRM was established in 2004. It provides a tool kit for suppliers and brands to use when implementing an RSL. Brands can have their own unique RSL or follow the RSL published by the American Apparel and Footwear Association (AAFA.) It can be downloaded at https://www.aafaglobal.org. Certifying bodies like Intertek and SGS are very familiar with testing for RSLs.

Here are some of the chemicals typically found in RSLs

- Carcinogenic aromatic amines
- Allergenic disperse dyes
- Heavy metals
- Organotins
- Chlorinated aromatics
- Flame retardants
- Formaldehyde
- Phthalates
- Auxiliary chemicals such as PFOS etc.

If you need help in Vietnam with testing for RSLs or developing your own RSL then I recommend you contact either Control Union, Intertek or SGS.

Certifying bodies in Vietnam

Control Union, SGS and Intertek are certifying bodies. They don't own any of the standards mentioned above; they certify compliant factories. They also test final products to make sure they meet the standards.

Intertek and SGS have fabric testing laboratories in Vietnam. They can test your fabric within 4 days. You will need to provide the color, fiber content, weight and fabric end-use. They will pick up your sample for free and, if you want it back, you pay for return delivery costs. They offer testing categories like:

- Shrinkage
- Color fastness
- Physical properties like tensile strength, pilling or pH
- Eco tests like Azo Dyes or Formaldehyde
- Care label verification

To quote you a price they need to know what to test. They will ask you for your buyers' manual. Companies like Walmart have buyers' manuals that contain RSLs and specify testing procedures. If you don't have a buyers' manual then you must tell Intertek or SGS exactly what to test for. Or, you can reference RSLs or standards like GOTS or Oeko Tex 100. You can also ask Intertek and SGS to develop your own buyers' manual by doing what they call protocol development.

If you are working with a factory that says they are GOTS, GRS or Oeko Tex certified, then you can hire Control Union, Intertek or SGS to do an independent unbiased check. Their job is to keep suppliers honest and protect your brand reputation. Here is contact information for certifying bodies in Vietnam:

Control Union

- Website: https://www.petersoncontrolunion.com
- Contact: Richard de Boer
- LinkedIn: https://www.linkedin.com/in/richard-de-boer-40bb9430/

SGS

- Website: https://www.sgs.vn
- Contact: Rob Parrish
- LinkedIn: https://www.linkedin.com/in/rob-parrish-72950/

Intertek

- Website: http://www.intertek.vn/contact/
- Contact: Silvia Dwi Febriani
- LinkedIn: https://www.linkedin.com/in/silvia-dwi-febriani-1536058a/

ADVANCES IN FABRIC DYEING

Worldwide, the apparel industry produces an astonishing 60 billion kilograms of fabric annually, using up to 9 trillion gallons of water for dyeing. We should have a basic understanding of fabric dyeing if we are buying and selling Eco fabrics. Here is a quick fabric dyeing primer and introduction to Eco dyeing technologies of the future.

Fabric dyeing steps

There are three steps to dyeing fabrics: preparation, dyeing and finishing.

Preparation removes unwanted impurities from the fabrics. This is achieved by cleaning the fabrics with aqueous alkaline substances and detergents or by applying enzymes. Many fabrics are bleached with hydrogen peroxide or chlorine in order to remove their natural color. If the fabric is to be sold white, optical brightening agents are added.

.   .   .

Dyeing involves soaking the yarn or fabric in water with dyes or pigments at various temperatures and pressures. There are over 10,000 different dyes and pigments. Dyes use colorants that are fully dissolved in water. Pigments use colorants that are solid particles suspended in water. A good analogy is salt water vs. tomato juice. During the dyeing step, chemicals such as surfactants, acids, electrolytes, carriers, leveling agents, promoting agents, chelating agents, emulsifying oils and softening agents are applied to the fabric to get uniform color and color fastness. The dyes or pigments must be infused into both the outer and inner surface of the fibers as much as possible.

Finishing involves treatments with chemicals which improve the quality of the fabric. Permanent press treatments, water proofing, softening, anti-static protection, soil resistance, stain release and microbial/fungal protection are all examples of fabric treatments applied in the finishing process.

Dyeing background and concerns

There are several types of dyes: natural dyes, synthetic dyes, food dyes and others. Until the middle of the nineteenth century, all the dyes used for fabrics were natural. In 1856 purple mauveine was the first synthetic dye to be discovered. William Henry Perkin, then age 18, was given a challenge by his professor to synthesize quinine. He tried and failed. Cleaning the flask with alcohol, Perkin noticed purple portions of the solution. The first synthetic dye was born. Since then there has been no looking back in the production of synthetic dyes; they are cheap, colorful, colorfast and easy to make.

The dyeing process uses a lot of water. In batch processing, the fabric is put into a big bath of water full of dye stuff. The fabric needs five to ten times its own weight in water to get good dye penetration. 200

million liters of dye-house waste water is released into the environment every year due to the inefficiency of the fabric dyeing process
and lack of effective water treatment.

Dye-house waste water pollutes because of color and toxic chemicals
like benzidine, naphthalene and other aromatic compounds. Azo
dyes are the biggest group of chemicals released into the environment due to fabric dyeing. Azo colorants can break apart to form
amines which are carcinogenic.

Heavy metals exist in dyes and end up in print and dye-house
waste water. Examples of heavy metals are titanium oxide, chro-
mate, molybdenum, and iron. Titanium oxide is used for pearles-
cent pigments. Aluminum and brass are used in metallic inks.
These metals become toxic when they react with other chemicals
naturally present in nature by forming poisonous soluble
compounds.

The greatest environmental concern with dye-house waste water is
color. Colored water blocks sunlight from getting through to microor-
ganisms below the surface. Algae, bacteria and plants need light to
grow and sustain the food chain. If light does not get below the
surface, then the circle of life becomes a straight line. Where's the
light at the bottom of the lake?

Eco dyeing technologies of the future

e.dye® sells colored polyester yarn in 2,500 different colors. Polyester
starts as chips of solid white wax. The wax is melted and squeezed
through the tiny holes to make polyester yarn. e.dye® adds color
chips during the melting phase so when the polyester yarn is
squeezed through tiny holes, it comes out as colored yarn. No water is

used. You can knit or weave the colored polyester yarn to get any color variations you want.

- Website: https://e-dye.com
- Contact: Michael Murphy
- LinkedIn: https://www.linkedin.com/in/michael-murphy-2468a794/

Newtech Textile colors your fabric by printing all over the fabric. Their technology, Cooltrans, prints on cotton, rayon, bamboo, linen, wool, nylon, polyester and silk. The printing process does not involve heat or water saving electricity and the environment. The only water involved is for finishing and the amount is the same as traditional finishing.

- Email: allen.lai@newtech-textile.com
- Website: www.newtech-textile.com

eCO2Dye has developed a waterless fabric dyeing process using carbon dioxide (CO_2) as the solvent for dyeing as opposed to water. Many conventional disperse dyes are soluble in CO2 at high temperatures and pressures. When polyester fabric is mixed with CO_2 and disperse dyes at high temperatures and pressure, polyester fabrics dye beautifully. This method reduces dye costs and eliminates the large amount of additives needed in conventional water dyeing.

- Website: http://eco2dye.com

Toyoshima is a Japanese textile trading company that created a fabric brand that focuses on using food colors. They use food waste to dye fabric. Food companies supply Toyoshima with segregated food waste that contain natural dyes. Toyoshima produces and dyes the fabric in eight food colors: cabbage, lettuce, spring onion, tomato, tea, onion, coffee and purple cabbage. For more information contact Mori.

- Email: mori@toyoshimala.com

Dyeing+ and Heifei Qian Herb Dyeing are two separate companies in China producing apparel and home textiles made with natural dyes. The plants they use are chebule dye for black, madder dye for red, radix arnebiae dye for purple, turmeric dye for yellow and radix isatidis dye for indigo. They control planting, extracting, dyeing, spinning, knitting and weaving. They dye cotton, wool, silk, hemp, modal, Tencel®, bamboo and rayon.

- Contact: Simon Chen
- Email: simon@plantsdyeing.com
- Website: www.plantsdyeing.com

- Email: herbdyeing@sacochina.com
- Website: www.herbdyeing.com

Some dye-houses use ultrasound-assisted textile dyeing. Shooting sound-waves at fabric while it is being dyed has many benefits. Clumps of chemicals with high relative molecular mass are broken into smaller pieces so that colorants can penetrate fibers faster and at lower temperatures - this saves energy. Gases trapped in fibers are released allowing dyes to infuse easier. The quantity of auxiliary chemicals needed is also reduced when you shoot ultra-sound waves at fabric during the dyeing process.

When determining if a fabric is Eco or not, dyeing technology and chemicals play a big role. If you start with organic cotton or traditional hemp then the dyeing process needs to be the highest degree of Eco possible as well.

6 ECO FABRIC WHOLESALERS

Dave Quach - Greenyarn - Vietnam

I met Dave at the Vietnam Textile and Garment Trade show in Ho Chi Minh City in 2015. He is focused on supplying the local market with Eco yarns. His parents were the first to import fabric into Vietnam post 1975; he is continuing his parents legacy with a focus on Eco. Greenyarn.vn was conceived during his studies in New Zealand where he experienced nature at its best. He has experience supplying organic cotton and recycled yarn in small MOQ for local brands. He specializes in melange yarns and aims to supply more Eco products as soon as the local demand picks up. Looking ahead to 2019 he is working with his supply chain to offer specialty yarns like constant temperature yarn, milk yarn and aloe vera yarn. Dave knows the local knitting and dyeing suppliers in Vietnam well.

- Email: Kienlan@greenyarn.vn
- Website: www.greenyarn.vn

Benjamin Itter - Lebenskleidung - Germany

I met Benjamin at the Ethical Fashion Show in Berlin in 2015. I visited his office and realized that he and his partners were Eco warriors down in the trenches. Their journey began in 2006 in India where they bought herbally dyed fabrics using ancient Ayuravedic methods leaving no environmental footprint and having a healing effect on the skin. After successfully producing Eco towels, in 2011 they started importing GOTS jersey fabrics from India to Germany.

They strive to innovate each year. They are experimenting with REFIBRA™. REFIBRA™ technology involves up-cycling cotton scraps from garment production to produce new fabrics. They also partnered up with a sustainable fashion brand for babies, Cotonea, to supply organic and fair trade fabrics from Uganda and Kyrgyzstan. These countries offer a wide range of organic wovens that Benjamin resales in small quantity.

Their main focus now is organic cotton knits such as jersey, french terry or interlock. They are expanding their range to include wool, silk, linen and vegetable tanned leather. They launch two fabric collections per year and their MOQ for most fabrics is 1 meter. They can provide sample fabric immediately and, if they don't have available stock, the production time is 8-10 weeks. 95% of their fabrics are certified according to GOTS.

- Email: ben@lebenskleidung.com
- Website: www.lebenskleidung.com

Paul King - Kendor Textiles - Canada

Paul started working for Kendor Textiles in the 1980s and bought the company with a Chinese partner in 2009. I met Paul at the Outdoor Retailer Show in Denver in 2018. Kendor Textiles started as a family owned business in the 1950s.

In 1992, when his first daughter was born, he reflected on the magnitude of pollution in the apparel industry and how it would affect her generation. He influenced Kendor management to push their suppliers to implement Eco standards and traceability. Thanks to his stewardship, Kendor started selling organic cottons, hemps, bamboos, and recycled polyester fabrics.

At a Planet Textile Forum in Shanghai he learned about the Sustainable Apparel Coalition and their Higg Index which motivated him to apply more pressure on his Chinese supply chains. Thanks to being proactive, his supply chain was not a victim of the Chinese government crackdown on polluting fabric mills in 2017.

He sells mostly knit fabrics out of his warehouse in Vancouver. He targets Eco minded people who want to know what they are buying and where it is coming from. His MOQ starts at 50 meters and his maximum order quantity is 1,000 meters. His typical lead time is 30 days. He stocks 180 different fabrics in greige which he can custom dye or print.

Paul's fabric is produced in China. He will do Asia to Asia business which means you can sample and order your fabric in Vancouver, it will be made in China, then the fabric will be shipped directly to your sewing factory in Vietnam.

- Email: paul@kendortextiles.com
- Website: www.kendortextiles.com

Patty Grossman - O Ecotextiles - USA

I found Patty and her sister, Leigh Anne, during my Eco research. They are based in the Seattle. They have an amazing blog explaining everything from endocrine disruptors to micro-plastics. Read their blog and you get a degree in Eco science.

They founded O Ecotextiles in 2004 and began a world-wide search for manufacturing partners. Their mission was to build a Cradle-to-Cradle Certified supply chain to create no-impact, perfectly safe, incredibly luxurious fabrics.

They began working with people around the world. They found a Romanian farmer who grows dew-retted hemp stalks. They befriended a Japanese mill owner committed to green processes. They sourced ozone instead of chlorine to bleach fabric. They discovered a 100-year-old Italian mill that produces no wastewater. Another Italian dye-house in their mix produces biodegradable and heavy-metal-free fabrics. In Chile they sniffed out a mill shifting to entirely green processes. They are worldly and have gotten down to the Eco roots.

Fast forward to 2018 and they are selling Eco fabrics for apparel, drapery, tabletops, upholstery and bedding.

- Email: service@twosistersecotextiles.com

- Website: www.twosistersecotextiles.com

Toyoshima - Orgabits - Japan

Toyoshima is a textile trading company based in Japan. I met them at the Sourcing at Magic Trade Show in Las Vegas in 2017. They specialize in supplying their own branded organic cotton called Orgabits. Their mission is to contribute to the global environment bit by bit and help expand the area of organic farms from 1% to 10% globally. They offer organic cotton yarn and fabric.

- Email: mori@toyoshimala.com

Vik Giri - Gallant - USA

I first met Vik at the Sourcing at Magic show in Las Vegas in 2017. His brand message was hyper focused and clear: "We specialize in organic cotton bags and apparel." His mission is to better the environment with sustainable products and improve the lives of those who are part of the production process.

Vik traveled around India to observe the challenges farmers face and see the condition of factory workers for himself. What he saw motivated him to start his business and become a champion of Fair Trade.

Vik offers organic cotton t-shirts and polos made with combed and ring-spun cotton procured from Chetna Organic Company. They manage a non-GMO organic cotton field. All products are completely traceable to the farm villages where the cotton was grown and harvested. All farmers receive fair trade prices. All the cotton is handled according to USDA standards and manufactured using GOTS standards certified by Control Union. He uses GOTS certified low impact dyes for printing. His t-shirts and polos are customizable to your color, size, shape, print, and sleeve length. If you need ready made Eco bags or apparel then check out Gallant International.

- Email: gallant@gallantintl.com
- Website: www.gallantintl.com

2 HEMP FACTORIES

Leon Xu - Hemp Fortex Industries - China

Leon started producing hemp fabric in China in 1994. He expanded into suppling organic cotton and recycled polyester. His GOTS certified factory has knitting, weaving, washing and sewing operations. The factory has been 100% solar powered since 2015. He has his own small hemp farm which is used for research and development. If you order a custom fabric, then the MOQ is 2,000 meters. If you order from their stock fabric then there is no MOQ. Nancy is the sales representative in the US and Joseph is the sales representative in China.

- Email: nancy@hempfortex.com (US)
- Email: joseph.zhang@hempfortex.com (China)
- Website: www.hempfortex.com

Jason Fung - China Hemp - China

Jason works for China Hemp which is a spinning mill that specializes in hemp yarns. He offers 42 different blends of hemp, cotton, Tencel® and modal in either compact yarn or combed yarn. The hemp community in China is small and everybody knows everybody. Jason can introduce you to fabric factories or sell you fabric directly.

- Email: jason.fung@chinahemp.com
- Website: http://www.chinahemp.com

3 RECYCLED POLYESTER FACTORIES

Chris Chen - Unifi - China

Unifi is the world leader in recycled polyester. The company was founded in 1971 in Greensboro, North Carolina. Their core business is producing synthetic fibers for the automotive, footwear, apparel, home furnishing, medical, socks and hosiery industries. They transform plastic bottles into flakes, resins and fibers of the highest quality and integrity. In 2007 they developed a branded recycled polyester fiber called REPREVE. In 2008 Unifi established a subsidiary in China. They produce recycled polyester in both the USA and China.

- Website: www.unifi.com
- LinkedIn: https://www.linkedin.com/in/chris-chen-88a79824

Nina Lin - Haili Green Fiber - China

Nina Lin works for Haili Green Fiber that produces 100% branded recycled polyester yarn called Rebo. Their company was founded in 2010. Their MOQ for recycled yarn is 8 tons.

- Email: ninalin@zjhaili.cn
- Website: www.hlrefiber.com

Nina can introduce you to her customers who are making a variety of fabrics using her yarn:

- Mr. Zhong Guo Qiang who makes outerwear fabric: xinruifangzhi@163.com.
- Kevin who makes backpack and luggage fabric: kevin@leejotex.com.cn.

Hu Xiao - Zhongxing Environmental - China

Zhongxing Environmental started spinning recycled polyester filament in China in 2012. They have many different products which you can see on their website.

- Email: huxiaolong@zxhb88.com
- Website www.zxhb88.com

1 RECYCLED COTTON SUPPLIER

Hisayuki Mori - Yagi - Japan

Yagi is a Japanese textile trading company that sells yarns, fabrics and garments. Yagi was founded in 1893 and has representative offices in China, Thailand, Bangladesh and Vietnam - one in Hanoi and one in Ho Chi Minh City. They have a branded recycled cotton yarn called Recycolor. They collect cut waste from sewing factories, ensuring uniform quality. Then they recycle the cut waste into beautiful melange yarn which they also make into fabric.

- Email: mori@toyoshimala.com
- Website: https://www.yaginet.co.jp

2 BAMBOO FACTORIES

Lina Grace - Tenbro - China

Tenbro is a leader in bamboo fiber production in China. Their unique selling point is that they have intellectual property rights accredited by the Chinese State Intellectual Property Bureau for various bamboo fiber production methods. They produce yarn and fabric using bamboo/modal, bamboo/lyocell and bamboo/charcoal. They also make bamboo fabrics blended with cotton and spandex. Their MOQ for stock fabrics is about 900 meters. Their MOQ for custom fabrics is 3,000 meters. Their website clearly shows all their bamboo yarns. Contact Lina if you want to buy Tenbro yarn. Contact Alex if you want to buy Tenbro fabric.

- Email: lina@tenbro.com (Yarn)
- Email: product01@tenbro.com (Alex, for fabric.)
- Website: www.tenbro.com

Bob Chang - Evai Bamboo - China

Bob works for Evai Bamboo. I met Bob at the Intertextile Trade Show in Shanghai in 2017. Evai had a beautiful and professional booth showcasing their bamboo fabrics, garments and towels. They knit, dye and finish their fabric in their own factory.

- Website: http://www.aiwayi.com.cn

3 RAYON FACTORIES

Michael Kininmonth - Lenzing - Austria

Lenzing is a world leader in cellulosic fibers. They started producing rayon in 1939, modal in 1965 and lyocell in 1997. In 2004 Lenzing acquired the trademark Tencel®. In 2007 they started producing in China. In 2016 they introduced REFIBRA™ which is lyocell fibers made from cut waste from cotton clothing factories. Lenzing is a leader in closed loop cellulosic regeneration using wood pulp from sustainably managed forests.

- LinkedIn: https://www.linkedin.com/in/michael-kininmonth-0536bb36/
- Website: www.lenzing.com

Chen Jieling - Baoding Swan Fiber - China

Baoding Swan Fiber started producing rayon in 1957. In 2014 they started producing lyocell which they branded as Oricell. They use closed loop cellulosic regeneration and use wood pulp from sustainably managed forests.

- Website: www.swanoricell.com
- LinkedIn: https://www.linkedin.com/in/chen-jieling-40825iba/

Jilin Chemical Fiber - China

Jilin Fiber produce rayon from wood pulp, cotton linters pulp and bamboo pulp. They have a patent for bamboo rayon called Tanboocel. They produce rayon staple fiber or filament.

- Website www.jlhxjt.com

6 ECO SEWING FACTORIES

Eric Fraboulet - Eco Bambou - Vietnam

Eco-Bambou is a French owned brand that manufactures for itself and other Eco-oriented brands. They specialize in Eco clothing and accessories for men, women and children. They offer bamboo, Tencel®, modal, coffee and soybean fabrics. They use Eco water-based pigment for printing.

Eric has been working in Vietnam for more than 20 years, producing garments. He uses waste fabric to make smaller items like baby socks, face masks and small size underwear. He produces cork purses and then uses the scrap cork to make trinkets like key holders. He converted all his hang tags cords from plastic to natural string fibers.

They produce 3,500 pcs per month for outside customers. If you use their existing fabrics then the MOQ is 20 pieces. If you want to develop your own fabric then the MOQ is 700 pieces. If you need a factory in Vietnam that is good at sourcing Eco fabrics then contact Eric through his website.

- Email: bambouproduction@yahoo.com
- Website: bamboucompany.com

Marian Van Rappard - Evolution3 - Vietnam

When I first met Marian I knew I was experiencing something extraordinary. He genuinely cares about the happiness of his workers and designed experiments to measure and improve their happiness. His factory has its own massage parlor, fruit bar and organic vegetable garden. Check out his Youtube video, Dawn Denim - Fair Wear to Love Affair.

Marian is from Germany and started working in Vietnam producing jeans for other brands. Then he established his own jeans factory called Evolution 3. He produces his own brand of jeans, Dawn Denim, and can produce jeans for you. All the cotton he uses is GOTS certified and he uses recycled polyester. His strength is design and development - no tech packs needed. His MOQ is 1,000 pieces.

- Email: marian@evolution3.com
- Website: www.evolution3.com

Paul Norriss - Un-Available - Vietnam

Un-Available started as fashion forward clothing brand based in London called Marshall Artists. Paul is one of the founders. Paul discovered quality manufacturing in Vietnam in 2000 and opened his own factory in 2002. Paul produces knit and woven premium streetwear fashion garments. He has in-house screen printing and provides exemplary customer service.

Paul's ethos is to be pro-active. He has implemented many Eco initiatives in his factory. He offers biodegradable poly bags, his canteen has no plastic straws and all plastic bottles used in the factory are recycled. Customers are offered fountain water instead of bottled water. LED lighting has been installed throughout the factory to reduce light energy by 38%. All AC units have been replaced with energy efficient inverters. He is investing in more expensive inks that dry in a shorter time to reduce the flash curers energy use. He is changing the sewing machinery to electric drive to save 35% energy. These are steps Paul is implementing to improve his energy efficiency and waste management.

- Email: paul.norriss@un-available.net
- Website: Un-Available.net

Benjamin Grépinet - Gingko - Vietnam

Ginkgo is an Eco fashion company established in Vietnam in 2007. It is managed by a team of French and Vietnamese. They design and produce their own tourist t-shirt collections and they can produce t-shirts for you too. Why the name Gingko? The ginkgo tree has Eco significance because it is the first plant that grew back after the 1945 bombing in Hiroshima.

Gingko offers knit and woven GOTS certified cotton fabrics. They source super fine SUPIMA cotton and they use quality spandex for blends. They offer a super soft cotton option that is sueded with a diamond emery technique. They can embroider and print your designs using low impact dyes.

- Email: neb@ginkgo-vietnam.com
- Website: www.ginkgo-vietnam.com

Vincent Djen - Cheng Kung Garments -China

Vincent is a fashion innovator, educator, and mentor. He cofounded an incubator called FashionEx and is the director of the Cheng Kung garment factory that produces woven outerwear for premium brands in Europe. The Cheng Kung factory was built by his parents in 1975. He describes himself as a fabric nerd. Sourcing innovative outerwear fabrics is his passion. He started Blackeyerags, a UK brand, with friends. He understands the whole fashion process from design through production to visual merchandising.

He works as a consultant and can connect you with Eco fabric supply chains in China. He recently developed a recycled polyester fabric that has mechanical stretch and water repellency weighing in at 110 gsm - great for spring outdoor jackets that he can produce for you.

- Email: wsdjen@chengkung.cn
- Website: www.chengkung.com

Mafalda Pinto - Scoop - Portugal

Mafalda founded SCOOP in Portugal in 1991 as a manufacturer of apparel. She specializes in casual and sportswear styles made with both knit and woven fabric. From the beginning she set clear goals to be Eco and achieves it through on-going education. SCOOP is ISO 9001, SA 8000 certified and listed on the Higg Index. Her factory layout uses the cell system allowing for small production runs. Her MOQ is 300 pieces. She imports organic cotton yarn from certified companies in India and weaves it in Portugal. She offers certified recycled polyester and lyocell fabric. She can assist you with design, development and production.

- Email: mafalda@scoop.pt
- Website: www.scoop.pt

TAKE AWAYS

100% Eco fabrics do not exist. There are fabrics more Eco than others and to what degree depends on decisions made by fabric producers. Decisions made by consumers also make a difference because if we buy more Eco fabric then more will be produced.

While the accounts of toxic chemical pollution and animal abuse are negative, the positive starts with people deciding to be aware and support Eco initiatives like the Sustainable Apparel Coalition and their Higg Index. If you are a manufacturer then choose technology that is the most Eco. If you are a middleman then buy from trusted Eco sources that you personally verified. If you are a consumer then challenge brands to be transparent about their supply chains and be willing to pay a little extra for Eco products. The positive is that we have choices and we all can act.

ABOUT THE AUTHOR

Hi, my name is Chris Walker. I was born in Los Angeles, California in 1970 and grew up in Germany. After graduating from Cal Poly San Luis Obispo, California with a physics degree I studied Spanish for a year in Madrid, Spain. Then I joined the US Navy as an electronic technician serving six years on a nuclear powered submarine based out of Honolulu, Hawaii. My experience took me to the Gulf of Mexico where I worked on offshore drilling rigs for another six years. Finally, I settled down in Vietnam to start a family and learn about apparel manufacturing overseas from the inside out. I'd like to meet you and hear your story. As my good friend Jared Meadors taught me, "everyone has their story."

UnLabel by Marc Ecko and Shoe Dog by Phil Knight are must reads if you are about to embark on overseas apparel production. Learn from those who went before you.

WHAT'S THE NEXT STEP?

May I ask you a few questions?

- What product do you want to produce in Vietnam?
- Do you have any specific factory requirements?
- Why manufacture in Vietnam vs China or India?
- Is your order quantity per item greater than 1,000?
- Do you have tech packs or technical specifications?

When I speak with you, these are the questions I will ask. Depending on your answers, I can prepare you and introduce you to factories in Vietnam.

Do you have your design ready but no tech pack or sample? Does $US 1,000 to get you from design to sample-in-hand for one style fit your budget? If I could introduce you to a company that helps you with design and development plus creates the pre-production sample for you, then would you be interested? If yes, then let's schedule a Calendly appointment to confirm you are ready to embark on what will be an exciting and challenging journey. I can also offer small MOQ production.

Schedule an appointment to speak with me here:
    https://calendly.com/vietnaminsider

If you have your tech pack and or sample ready and just want to be introduced to factories then I can do that too. I charge a small fee per factory introduction. Contact me for details.

Here are other services I offer:

- Consulting
- Techpack creation services
- Factory introductions by email
- Factory visits
- Get a price quote
- Quality control
- Product development support
- Factory assessments
- Staff recruiting
- Office space rental

Share your story with me!

I'd like to give back by posting your story to my social media channels. Send me a well written piece about you and your brand. Plus, send a couple of cool pictures and I will review. If appropriate then I will share your story with my network. I wish you success. Thanks again for buying and reading my book. I hope to see you in Vietnam!

The End.

Printed in Great Britain
by Amazon